Beginners Handbook an
and Fi
2020 Edition

MW01295966

Table of Contents

Disclaimer

Information within this document is based on research from Paul Borosky, MBA., Doctoral Candidate. This information is for educational purposes. Our recommendations and analysis are the opinions and works of the author. We do not guarantee that all the information included is accurate. Make sure to conduct additional research and analysis before making investment decisions.

Acknowledgments

The motivation and drive to write this assessment were in no small part, due to my wonderful wife, Tishauna, kids, Cara, Katy, Maggie, and Paul Jr., stepson, Jayden and parents.

Forward

Reading and understanding financial statements and financial ratios is a critical skill needed by investors, finance students, accounting students, and business students. Without this skill, investors are left with selecting stocks based on 'water-cooler' conversations or because they like the company name – not a great foundation to build a retirement portfolio.

As for students, without a solid foundation with understanding financial statements, specifically, the income statement and balance sheet, and financial ratios, passing basic business courses will prove exceptionally difficult.

This leads to the purpose of the book.

This book was written to teach investors, business students, finance students, and accounting students about basic and advanced accounting and finance concepts and to apply the concepts in analyzing five consecutive years' of financial statements and financial ratios.

Book and Chapter Structures

This book was structured to help investors and students quickly and efficiently learn to read, understand, and use a company's income statement, balance sheet, and popular financial ratios for financial analysis and investment purposes.

Financial Statements – The income statement and balance sheet sections start with a brief explanation of each financial statement. With this foundation set, I then define, graph, and offer analysis tips and examples for each financial statement line item, such as revenues and long-term debt.

Financial Ratios – This section starts with showing formulas for popular financial ratios and also calculated financial ratios for five years, based on our example financial statements provided. Each financial ratio is then defined, formulas provided, calculations for the ratios illustrated, financial analysis tips offered, ratios graphed, covering a five-year time frame, in most cases, and brief analysis of the ratios.

Important financial ratios defined, calculated, and analysis tips offered includes the current ratio, cash ratio, quick ratio, net working capital ratio, total asset turnover ratio, fixed asset turnover ratio, days sales outstanding, inventory turnover, accounts receivable turnover, working capital turnover, accounts payable turnover, return on assets, return on equity, profit margin, gross profit margin, and several more.

In the end, hopefully, you will have a better understanding of financial statements and financial ratios in general.

About the Author

Paul Borosky, MBA., Doctoral Candidate, lives in the Orlando, FL. area and is the owner of Quality Business Plan, Tutor4Finance, EnjoyFloridaToday.com, and FinanceHomeworkHelp.net. His time is mostly spent with his family, business plan writing, writing books, financial modeling, and cruising. Oh, so many cruises.

Paul is obsessed with finance and entrepreneurship. As a child, he would traverse the neighborhood looking for side jobs, cutting grass, raking leave, almost anything for a couple of bucks. His first run-in with finance was as a mortgage broker in the mid-1990s. His fascination with finance led to an MBA with numerous credits in different finance courses.

To date, Paul has helped create two finance curriculums for a local college, teaches finance for a local college, considered a subject matter expert in finance, and has published numerous books on starting businesses, raising funds for small companies, passing finance courses, and analyzing company financial statements and financial ratios.

In the future, he intends to write extensively related to business plans, financial analysis, vacationing, strategic planning, corporate finance, and incorporating financial modeling into a startup or expanding organizations.

Financial Statements

The heart of this book, as you probably already guessed, based on the title, is to provide you with the tools and knowledge to do an in-depth analysis of a company's financial statements, as well as, its financial ratios, based on their 10K financial filing. For our examples, I use Darden's summarized financial statements and ratios for all samples.

With that said, in starting this chapter, we will first define and briefly analyze the income statement. Once complete, we will do a brief overview of the balance sheet. Finally, we get really crazy and start examining a multitude of financial ratios as they apply to Disney.

Income Statement

An income statement is one of several financial statements public companies are required to share with investors and other stakeholders. Critical aspects of the income statement include revenues, cost of goods sold (COGS), various expenses, taxes, and finally, the coveted net income.

When analyzing financial statements, especially the income statement, essential details to seek out would be trends. Trends, in financial analysis, are events that happen over time. For example, if revenues fall for an organization for two, or more, consecutive periods, this would be a trend, specifically, a concerning trend.

Unfortunately, there is no one specific trend to look for when analyzing financial statements. However, there is a professional process analysis follow in sniffing out trends. When analyzing financial statements, try searching for unusual changes. I don't mean to be vague. Analyzing financial statements takes practice, patience, and persistence.

Sample Income Statement:

Sample					
Income Statement 2018					
	2018	2017	2016	2015	2014
Revenues	8,080	7,170	6,933	6,764	6,285
COGS	2,303	2,070	2,039	2,085	1,892
Gross Profit	5,777	5,100	4,894	4,679	4,393

SG&A	409	387	384	430	413
Depreciation	313	272	290	319	304
R & D	-	-	-	-	-
Other	-	-	-	-	
Operating Expenses	7,313	6,492	6,311	6,396	5,976
EBIT	766	677	622	175	174
Other Income					
Interest Expense	161	40	172	192	134
EBT	605	637	450	175	174
Taxes	2	154	90	(21)	(9)
Net Income	**596**	**479**	**375**	**709**	**286**

Revenues

Warren Buffett once said if I remember correctly, that he could have the net income on an income statement reflect whatever number he pleased, within reason, legally. This thought should be very concerning for investors and other stakeholders who rely on the income statement for investment purposes. The only exception that he noted was that of the revenues.

Definition:

The revenue line item is a great starting point for us. Revenues are funds received by the company for products or services rendered.

In other words:

Revenues are the dollar amount of products or services a company sold to customers in the noted timeframe.

Analysis Tips:

As you can imagine, as investors, we want a company's revenues to increase continually. However, this increase should be, optimally, at a moderate pace. Substantial fluctuations, increasing or decreasing, indicates upheaval within the organization. For example, significant increases in revenue, over a short time, requires organizations to ramp up operations to meet the needs. In some instances, quality may suffer.

In contrast, significant declines in revenues show the firm is not performing well on the sales front. Either way, additional research is warranted when elevated risk is present. The elevated risk is the fluctuation, significantly, in revenues.

Revenues					
Revenues and Growth					
	2018	2017	2016	2015	2014
Revenues	8,080	7,170	6,933	6,764	6,285
Revenue Growth	12.7%	3.4%	2.5%	7.6%	N/A

Analysis:

In this sample, revenues started 2015 at approximately $6.28 billion. As of 2018, revenues had increased to roughly $8.08 billion. In terms of revenue growth, their year-over-year average, for the last four years, has been 6.5%. As compared to the industry, this is well above average. Further, the most significant growth has come in the last year. This indicates that the firm may be trending towards higher revenue growth in the future.

Expenses

As a rule, I like to analyze costs as a percentage of revenues. What I mean by this is that I divide the specific costs, such as cost of goods sold, by the revenues. This will give us how much the company spent on raw materials, as a percent of sales. By using percentages in this fashion, it is relatively easy to identify trends for expenses.

Cost of Goods Sold (COGS)

The cost of goods sold is always located directly below revenues on an income statement if the line item is needed at all. Keep in mind; some service-based companies will not include, nor need to add, the cost of goods sold line item.

Definition:

The cost of goods sold is how much money the company needed to spend on raw material, which is parts or items required to make their finished product, in the last year.

In other words:

If we manufactured bicycles, then the parts needed to build a bike, such as tires, pedals, and a flashy, squeezable horn, would be our cost of goods.

Analysis Tips:

When analyzing the cost of goods, make sure to compare the line item with revenues, as shown below. If the cost of goods, as a percentage, increases, then this indicates that the company's raw materials are costing more money AND the company is not recuperating the cost by increasing prices for customers. In other words, raw material prices are escalating, and the cost increase is not being passed on to the customer.

If the cost of goods percentage, as compared to revenues, decreases, then the company may be doing a better job negotiating prices for raw material. Kudos to the managers.

In a perfect world, we would love to see the cost of goods stay relatively consistent, as compared to revenues. This shows that there is little deviation in raw material costs for the company.

COGS as % of Revenues					
Income Statement 2018					
	2018	2017	2016	2015	2014
Revenues					

	8,080	7,170	6,933	6,764	6,285
COGS	2,303	2,070	2,039	2,085	1,892
COGS % Revenues	28.5%	28.9%	29.4%	30.8%	30.1%

Analysis:

In 2014, cost of goods sold was approximately 30.1% of revenues. As of 2018, this has declined to 28.5% of revenues. Further, this trend has been consistent for the last four years. This indicates that the organization is doing a better job negotiating prices with vendors. If the firm can maintain this trend, then more funds will be available for other costs or future dividends.

Selling, General, and Administrative Expenses (SG&A)

Selling, general, and administrative expenses are almost always referred to as SG&A on the income statement. This section reflects how much the company spent on costs that are not directly related to production, such as office supplies, advertising, and other similar, indirect expenses.

In other words:

All companies have overhead. The overhead may include advertising costs, office supplies costs, or rent/lease payments. These types of costs will be included in this line item.

Analysis Tips:

An essential consideration for SG&A is that these costs are directly controlled by management. If the costs increase/decrease substantially, as compared to sales, then we can possibly directly correlate managerial efficiencies or inefficiencies as a possible cause. Another way of saying this is that if SG&A looks terrible, then we can blame the management team.

When analyzing SG&A, comparing this line item with revenues is an excellent practice. If the organization increases revenues, while maintaining a steady SG&A, then the organization is increasingly optimizing its asset usage.

In contrast, if this line item starts to increase faster than sales, then the organization may not be optimally using its advertising and other resources.

SG&A as % of Revenues Income Statement 2018					
	2018	2017	2016	2015	2014
Revenues	8,080	7,170	6,933	6,764	6,285
SG&A	409	387	384	430	413
SG&A % Revenues	5.1%	5.4%	5.5%	6.4%	6.6%

Analysis:

In this example, SG&A has been trending lower for the last five years. In 2014, SG&A was 6.6% of revenues. The statistic had steadily decreased to 5.1% of revenues in 2018. This indicates that the company is generating more revenues using fewer overhead costs. Unfortunately, this trend is not sustainable. Further decline in this area may substantially hinder quality control, research and development, and other indirect, yet, essential aspects of operations due to budget cuts.

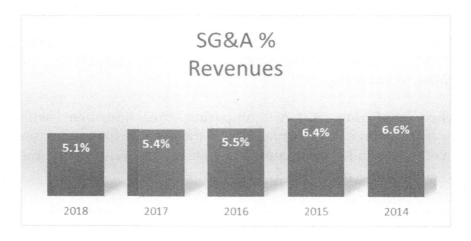

Research and Development (R&D)

Research and development are funds spent on exploring new products and services. Spending money on research and development is critical for almost all companies because of the need to continually service and meet the needs and expectations of their customers.

In other words:

If a company wants to stay relevant, invest in innovation. R&D is the starting point for this process.

Analysis Tips:

When evaluating research and development, depending on the industry, my preference is to have research and development spending continually rising, regardless, of the revenue flow. This is because as a company grows, they inevitably sell more and more products and services. From this, improving and expanding upon these products and services should be an ever-increasing cost. Without doing this, companies may fall victim to obsolescence.

R & D					
Research and Development					
	2018	2017	2016	2015	2014
R & D	36.0	34.0	33.0	30.0	25.0
Growth	5.9%	3.0%	10.0%	20.0%	N/A

Analysis:

The R&D started 2014 strong. However, in subsequent years, the company's investments in R&D have diminished substantially. Without fully funding research and development, the company may fall behind with innovations.

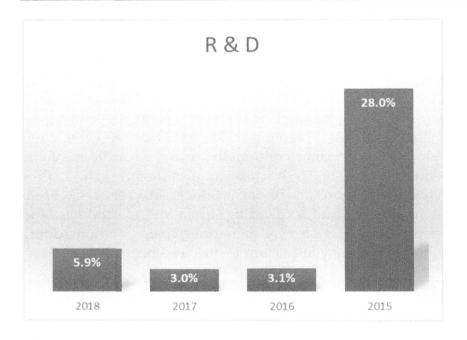

Operating Expenses

Operating expenses are costs that an organization incurs when conducting their normal daily operations.

In other words:

When a company is performing its services or creating their products, they incur specific costs, such as labor, electric, and other directly related costs to their operations.

Analysis Tips:

Operating expenses are often compared to revenues. If an organization can decrease its operating expenses, while making more money, then the organization is becoming more efficient. In contrast, if a company is increasing its operating costs at a faster pace than sales; then the company is either cutting their prices or not performing as efficiently as in previous years. From this, comparisons should be made with revenues, as well as with, industry competitors.

Operating Expenses					
	2018	2017	2016	2015	2014
Operating Expenses	7,313.0	6,492.0	6,311.0	6,396.0	5,976.0
% of Sales.	90.5%	90.5%	91.0%	94.6%	95.1%

Analysis:

This example indicates that the firm spends a significant portion of their revenues on operating costs. As a result, little funds may be left for new projects or dividend payments.

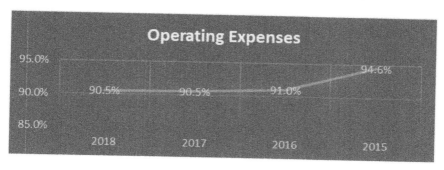

Earnings Before Interest and Taxes (EBIT)

The earnings before interest and taxes, commonly known as EBIT, is the company's operating profits.

In other words:

Based on operations alone, this is how much profit the organization is making.

Analysis Tips:

Financial analysts prefer to see steady growth in the EBIT. Further, comparing this line item with sales growth is also an excellent financial analysis practice. If the EBIT is growing faster as compared to sales, then, the company may be cutting costs to increase profits. When sales growth outpaces EBIT, this may mean the company is reducing its sales price to increase sales volume. If this is the case, the sales volume increase is actually detrimental to profits. Or at least profit growth.

EBIT Earnings Before Interest and Taxes					
	2018	**2017**	**2016**	**2015**	**2014**
EBIT	766.0	677.0	622.0	175.0	174.0
EBIT Growth	13.1%	8.8%	255.4%	0.6%	N/A
Sales Growth	12.7%	3.4%	2.5%	7.6%	N/A

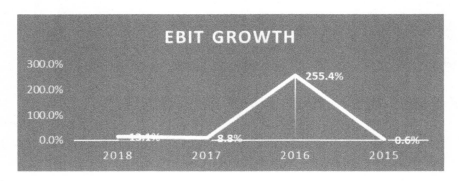

Interest Expense

Interest expense is how much a company has paid in interest to lenders or bondholders in a specific time frame. The benefit of using debt is that interest expense payments are usually tax-deductible. A challenge with high-interest expenses, or debt, is, in times of recession, affording high-interest expense payments may be difficult for a company to handle. With this said, high-interest expense line items may inevitably lead to financial insolvency.

In other words:

Having some interest expense on an income statement is suitable for a company. However, too much debt, or interest expense, may cause undue hardship in times of recession.

Analysis Tips:

Investors usually like to see at least some interest expense. This shows that the firm is using borrowed funds to make money. This practice is fantastic concerning increasing return on equity for investors. Hoot Hoot! A dramatic decrease in this line item shows that the company paid off a significant amount of debt. Usually, as we all know, reduced debt can be a good thing.

In contrast, a significant rise in interest expense indicates that the company is taking on an exceptional amount of debt. In doing this, the company is simultaneously increasing the risk for the organization.

Interest Expense				
Interest Expense				
2018	2017	2016	2015	2014

Interest Expense	161.0	40.0	172.0	192.0	134.0
Growth	302.5%	-76.7%	-10.4%	43.3%	N/A

Analysis:

Over the last five years, the interest expense has fallen from a peak of 192 million to a, possibly, more manageable 161 million. If this trend continues, then the firm will increasingly become less risky for investors.

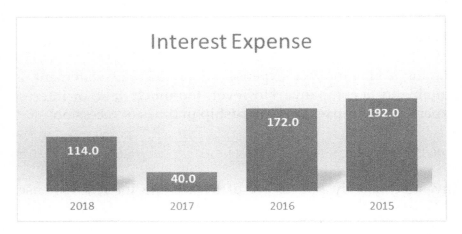

Earnings Before Taxes (EBT)

Earnings before taxes mean that after interest payments are deducted from profits, the remaining balance is taxable income.

In other words:

This is the dollar amount that the company expects to pay in taxes.

Analysis Tips:

Earnings before taxes (EBT) is a critical line item because of our need to calculate the expected tax rate for a company. Other than that, this line item, from an analyst perspective, is not that important.

Earnings Before Taxes					
	2018	**2017**	**2016**	**2015**	**2014**
EBT	605.0	637.0	450.0	175.0	174.0
Growth	-5.0%	41.6%	157.1%	0.6%	N/A

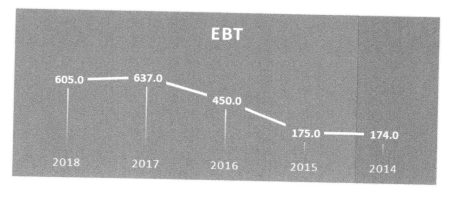

Taxes

The tax line item is how much money the company expects to pay government agencies in taxes. Of course, the more taxes a company pays, the fewer profits afterward. So, investors and financial analysts want to see a low dollar amount on this line item.

In other words:

Investors and analysts love to see companies paying as little taxes as possible. This is simply because whatever money that is left after taxes are spent is profits for the company.

Analysis Tips:

Not much to analyze here. As I said, we definitely want to see this line item as low as possible.

Taxes Paid					
	2018	2017	2016	2015	2014
Taxes	62.0	154.0	48.0	19.0	18.0
Growth	-59.7%	220.8%	152.6%	5.6%	N/A

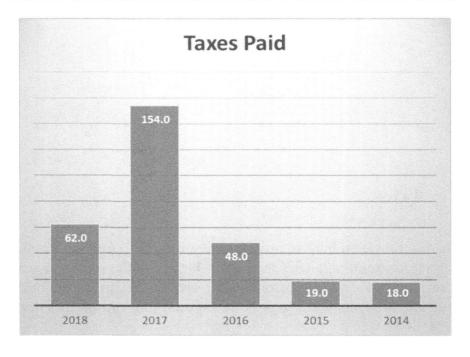

Net income

The net income is how much funds are available to the company, after operational costs, interest expenses, and taxes are paid. The funds from net income may be used in two ways. First, the company may distribute all, or some, of the net income to shareholders through dividend payments.

A second choice for using net income funds would be to reinvest the money back into the company. When doing this, the company may be able to take on additional projects without needing external financing.

In other words:

The net income is the profits a company has available to either reinvest or compensate investors through dividend payouts.

Analysis Tips:

The net income is one of the most popular line items analyzed by investors and financial analysts. This is because, as noted above, the net income is the amount of money that could possibly be paid out in dividends or used to grow the company. Either way, investors know that a higher and growing net income inevitably will lead to higher stock prices or dividend payouts.

Net Income					
Net Income Growth					
	2018	2017	2016	2015	2014
Net Income	596	479	375	709	286

Net Income Growth	24.4%	27.7%	-47.1%	147.9%	N/A

Analysis:

The company ended 2014 with a net income of 286 million. In 2015, their net income exploded to $709 million. This represented a 147.9% increase. A critical factor for this drastic increase was related to their taxes. It seems like the company had a tax credit of approximately $21 million. Over the last two years, the firm has had moderate net income growth of about 27.7% and 24.4% respectively. This shows that the firm is trending higher in relation to net income and net income growth.

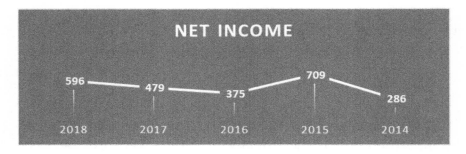

Tax Rate

The tax rate is how much the company expects to pay in taxes, as a percentage. This calculation can only be done by reviewing the income statement. To calculate the tax rate, divide taxes by EBT, or earnings before taxes. From an investor standpoint, this calculation may not be earth-shatteringly necessary. However, for our calculations related to valuation and weighted average cost of capital, the tax rate is critical.

In other words:

The tax rate is the percentage of taxes paid as compared to earnings before taxes. As we all know, the lower the tax bill, the more money for profits.

Analysis Tips:

When analyzing the tax rate, financial analysts prefer to see a stable tax rate percentage. Usually, for large corporations, a tax rate between 16 to 22% is expected.

Tax Rate					
Tax Rate 2018					
	2018	2017	2016	2015	2014
Tax Rate	10.2%	24.2%	10.7%	10.9%	10.3%

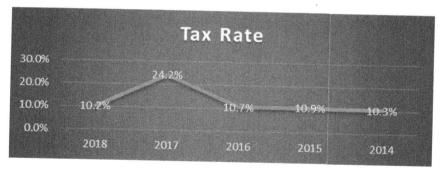

Balance Sheet

A balance sheet depicts, or shows, a company's financial standing at a specific point in time. In other words, the balance sheet will tell investors and other stakeholders, how much money, equipment, etc. that a firm has at a specific point in time.

For analysis purposes, essential line items that need to be reviewed would include cash, inventory, Accounts Receivable on the asset side of the balance sheet. As for the liability and equity side, the main items would consist of accounts payable, notes payable, and long-term debt.

Balance Sheet Sample

Sample					
Balance Sheet					
	2018	2017	2016	2015	2014
Cash	146	233	274	535	98
Short Term Investment	-	-	-	-	-
Account Receivable	83	75	64	78	84
Inventory	205	178	175	163	197
Other	-	-	-	-	-

Current Assets	553	587	820	**1,056**	**1,976**
Net PPE	2,429	2,272	2,041	3,215	3,381
Goodwill	1,183	1,201	872	872	873
Other	-	-	-	-	-
Total Assets	**5,469**	**5,292**	**4,583**	**5,995**	**7,101**
Accounts Payable	277	249	242	199	233
Accrued Expense	177	149	135	141	126
Accrued Taxes	-	2	-	13	-
Notes Payable	-	-	-	-	208
LT Debt - Current	-	-	-	15	15
Other	-	-	-	-	-
Total Current Liabilities	1,384	1,289	1,187	1,197	1,619
LT Debt	926	936	440	1,452	2,481
Other	-	-	-	-	-
Total Liabilities	**3,274**	**3,190**	**2,630**	**3,661**	**4,944**
Common Stock	1,631	1,614	1,502	1,405	1,302
Treasury	(8)	(8)	(8)	(8)	(8)
Retained					

Earnings	658	560	548	1,026	996
Other	-	-	-	-	-
Total Equity	2,195	2,102	1,952	2,334	2,157
Total Equity & Liability	5,470	5,292	4,583	5,995	7,101

Cash

The cash position for the company is vital to evaluate because, just like individuals, a company needs money to pay expenses, both near and long-term. Essential trends to look out for, concerning cash on the balance sheet, would be a continuous decline in cash or significant increases.

A cash declining trend may indicate the company is spending more money than it is taking in. As for cash increases, this could mean that the firm is running out of new, profitable projects to start, AND the executive team does not want to pay out dividends to investors. This could be fertile grounds for activist investors to start acquiring market shares and possibly force dividend payments.

Analysis Tips:

For analysis purposes, not only do I like to evaluate a company's cash position in terms of dollars, but also as a percentage of sales and a percentage of total assets.

Cash as a % of Sales
Balance Sheet

	2018	2017	2016	2015	2014
Cash	146	233	274	535	98
% of Sales	1.8%	3.2%	4.0%	7.9%	1.6%
% of Total Assets	2.7%	4.4%	6.0%	8.9%	1.4%

Analysis:

For this firm, they started 2014 with approximately $98 million in cash. The cash position has grown $146 million in 2018. In relation to sales and total assets, the significant fluctuation between both comparables indicates that neither sales nor total assets are benchmarks used for the executive team to assess their cash needs. With this said, a better way to analyze their cash position would be through the use of financial ratios, specifically the current ratio and quick ratio.

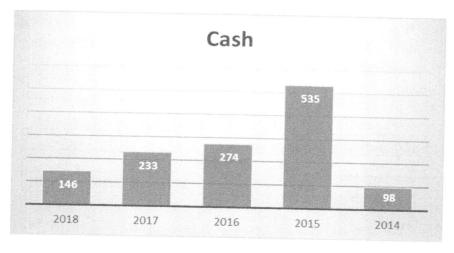

Short-Term Investments

Short-term investments are located in the current asset section of the balance sheet. This line item shows the amount of funds a company expects to receive from investments within the next 12 months. Short-term investment usage is an excellent practice for companies when they have a significant amount of cash. This allows a company to earn money on extra cash.

In other words:

Instead of leaving cash sitting in a checking account, earning no interest, by using short-term investments, this allows the company to at least generate some type of cash flow from excess cash that a company is holding.

Analysis Tips:

Any time a company uses short-term investments, this indicates excess cash. On the plus side, we can almost certainly rule out insolvency for the near term. As for a challenge, the organization may better serve its investors by dispersing excess cash through dividend payments.

Short-term Investments as a % of Sales and Total Assets					
Balance Sheet					
	2018	2017	2016	2015	2014
Short-Term Investment	31	28	30	19	20
% of Sales	0.4%	0.4%	0.4%	0.3%	0.3%
% of Total Assets	0.6%	0.5%	0.7%	0.3%	0.3%

Analysis:

The company has minimal short-term assets, as compared to total assets. Since the company's current assets are well below their current liabilities, this indicates that the firm has very little extra cash available for investing. Hell, some might even say the company is borderline insolvent.

Accounts Receivables

Accounts Receivable is the dollar amount that a company is expected to receive for products sold to suppliers or customers. In other words, the company has already shipped its products and is now awaiting payment. The longer it takes for the company to collect accounts receivable, the fewer funds available to run the company.

In other words:

Accounts Receivable is equivalent to going out to dinner at our favorite restaurant and receiving our meal. The period between receiving our meal and paying our check would be considered an account receivable for the restaurant.

Analysis Tips:

As investors, we want to see a low accounts receivable dollar amount. The lower the accounts receivables, the more cash the company will have to fund operations. In terms of analysis, a popular strategy for analyzing accounts receivable is to compare the line item with sales. If accounts receivable percentage is declining, as compared to sales, year over year, then the organization is collecting their accounts receivable at a faster pace. In other words, the company is turning its accounts receivable into cash quicker.

In contrast, an increasing percentage, as compared to sales, shows that the firm is taking longer to collect money due. This could possibly lead to cash shortages, depending on the company's cash position.

Accounts Receivable as a % of Sales					
Balance Sheet					
	2018	**2017**	**2016**	**2015**	**2014**
Accounts Receivables	83	75	64	78	84
% of Sales	1.0%	1.0%	0.9%	1.2%	1.3%

Analysis:

Our sample company's account receivable ended 2014 at $84 million. Further, this was 1.3% of sales. As of 2018, the revenues were about the same. However, the firm was able to reduce its accounts receivable, as a percentage of sales, to 1.0%. This indicates that the company has become more efficient in collecting its debt. Not only does this help cash flow, this also assists with improving working capital.

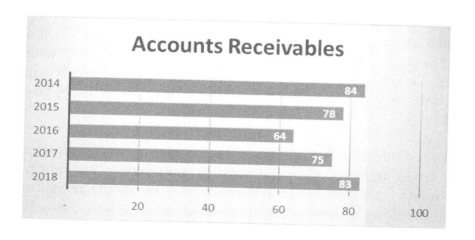

Inventory

Inventory is the dollar amount of finished, or unfinished (raw material), products that a company offers for sale, but has not sold. Controlling inventory is a crucial managerial practice to ensure optimal profits.

If a company holds to much inventory, then they risk obsolescence. In other words, if the company has too many items of a product, if a new product model comes out, then the firm may not be able to sell older models.

In contrast, if an organization does not have enough inventory, they risk a sellout. By doing this, the organization cannot sell additional products. Not only does this limit revenues, but it also really pisses off your customers.

Analysis Tips:

When attempting to analyze inventory, comparisons to sales and total assets are in order. By comparing inventory with total assets and sales, investors can determine if an organization is increasing or decreasing their inventory holdings.

If an organization is decreasing their inventory holdings, then this may indicate that the firm is optimizing its supply channels. An increase in inventory may mean the products are not selling as well as executives had hoped.

Inventory as a % of Sales and Total Assets					
Balance Sheet					
	2018	2017	2016	2015	2014
Inventory	205	178	175	163	197
% of Sales	2.5%	2.5%	2.5%	2.4%	3.1%
% of Total Assets	3.7%	3.4%	3.8%	2.7%	2.8%

Analysis:

The organization started in 2014 with an inventory position of $197 million. This position increased to $205 million in 2018. In reviewing the percent of sales comparison and total asset comparison with inventory (Shown below), the firm seems to align their inventory position with percent of sales. Further, the company appears to be declining their inventory position with sales. In other words, the company is holding less inventory as sales increase. This is fantastic because it shows the company is maximizing its inventory usage. However, if the firm is consistently selling out of products, then sales will inevitably be detrimentally impacted. You can't sell something you don't have. Common sense to you and me, not so much for some companies.

Current Assets

Current Assets are assets that a company either has in cash or can easily be converted into cash within a 12-month time frame. For example, popular current asset line items include cash, accounts receivable, inventory, and short-term investments. For the most part, a company will convert accounts receivables into cash within 30 to 90 days. As for inventory, depending on the industry, the company should turn over, or sell through, their inventory within 12 months. Finally, short-term investments are classified as investment vehicles that will mature within 12-months. When this investment vehicle matures, then the company can convert the securities to cash.

Current assets are significant for investors to analyze for the simple fact that a company needs cash to cover its debts or current liabilities. Specifically, an organization needs enough cash to cover its current liabilities. With this said, comparing current assets with current liabilities is always a great place to start when analyzing ratios. However, concerning a professional financial statement review, the right place to begin with analyzing current assets is by looking at the growth trend and its comparison to total assets.

In other words:

Current assets are money that the company has, or items, such as inventory and accounts receivable, that will turn into cash within 12 months.

Analysis Tips:

When analyzing current assets, first start by taking a look at the historical trend. Are current assets increasing or decreasing? If the current assets are growing, the company is holding more money for operations continuously. This is acceptable to ensure liquidity. If current assets are decreasing, then the organization may be running out of money. This is not always the case. However, as investors, this should be a definite red flag.

Next, take a look at your current liabilities, are they increasing or decreasing? If the current liabilities are growing, while current assets are shrinking, then the firm may be facing a liquidity crisis in the near term. If current assets and current liabilities are increasing and decreasing in tandem, then management is just keeping the two spreadsheet line items aligned — an excellent managerial practice.

A second trend to look for is whether the current assets, as a percentage of total assets, is increasing or decreasing. If current asset percentages are falling, while total assets are growing, this may mean that the company is optimizing its current asset utilization. This practice allows the firm to focus on long-term growth while using as little money in operations as possible. The strategy is excellent for highly utilizing money. However, in the event of a revenue slow down, the organization may face a cash shortage.

Current Assets as a % of Total Assets				
Balance Sheet				
	2018	2017	2016	2015	2014
Current Assets	553	587	820	1,056	1,976
% of Total Assets	10.1%	11.1%	17.9%	17.6%	27.8%
Growth	-5.8%	-28.4%	-22.3%	-46.6%	N/A

Analysis:

With this company, the firm had current assets of $1.9 billion in 2014. This number dropped to 553 million in 2018. This indicates that the company is shifting its assets away from liquidity to more long-term usage. For example, the company might be using cash to purchase equipment or properties. In this case, the company does seem to be increasing their property, plant, and equipment as their current assets decrease. The challenge with this strategy may be that the firm could run into a liquidity crisis if the economy goes south. More likely though, the organization is more focused on growth, and they are confident that revenues and cash flow will continue to grow in the foreseeable future.

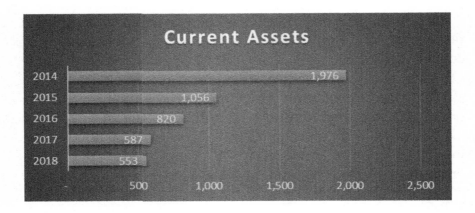

Property, Plant, and Equipment (PP&E)

As evident in the name, property, plant, and equipment, this balance sheet item indicates the book value of a firm's property, plant, and equipment. When assessing PP&E, historical trends are often best to analyze.

In other words:

Property, plant, and equipment represent fixed assets, or buildings and large pieces of equipment that an organization owns. In most cases, PP&E will be net PP&E. This means that depreciation has been subtracted from the property, plant, and equipment.

Analysis Tips:

When analyzing property, plant, and equipment, start with reviewing the historical trend. If the organization is continually increasing its property, plant, and equipment, then this means the firm is growing and purchasing more buildings and equipment to support production-related aspects of the business.

A second trend to examine is comparing PP&E with sales. If PP&E is staying steady, year over year, while sales are increasing, then the organization is generating and selling more products with the same amount of fixed assets. This is fantastic.

In contrast, if sales are dropping and property, plant, and equipment are holding steady, then the firm is not utilizing its fixed assets optimally. If this is the case, the firm should consider selling assets to better align its property, plant, and equipment with sales.

PP&E as a % of Sales				
Balance Sheet				
2018	2017	2016	2015	2014
PP&E				
2,429	2,272	2,041	3,215	3,381
% of Sales				
33.2%	35.0%	32.3%	50.3%	56.6%
Growth				
6.9%	11.3%	-36.5%	-4.9%	N/A

Analysis:

In 2016, the firm seemed to have divested a significant, approximately 35%, amount of their PP&E. This may have been aligned with the sale of their Red Lobster unit. Since 2016, the company has been increasing its PP&E. This shows that the firm is either replacing/remodeling their restaurants and equipment, or the company is opening new locations. Either way, investment in property, plant, and equipment is a great way to generate long-term growth in revenues.

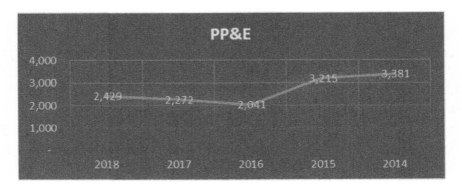

Total Assets

Total assets include, literally, everything, in terms of dollars, that a company owns. Further, total assets are funded by either debt or equity. Thus, the birth of the accounting equation, which is:

$$Assets = Liabilities + Equity$$

When analyzing total assets, financial analyst reviews historical trends, as well as, compare total assets with sales. Historical trends are essential to examine because a company may significantly increase or decrease their total assets. When this happens, for the most part, executives have made a strategic business change, which needs to be identified and assessed. This change may include selling a portion of their company or acquiring a different firm. No matter. This strategic change needs to be identified and examined.

As for comparing total assets with sales, this is critical from an operations perspective. If an organization can increase its revenues, while maintaining total assets, then the firm is generating more money with the same amount of money invested. This means that the company is becoming more efficient — a vital trait for investors to identify.

In other words:

Total assets are all of the assets that a company uses to make money. If total assets are increasing and sales are decreasing, then the company is using more money to make less money. Not a great strategy. Conversely, if the company is making more money and using the same or less money to do it, hoot, hoot, well done.

Analysis Tips:

When analyzing total assets, first start with looking at the historical trend. If the company is continually increasing its total assets, year-over-year, then the organization is growing to meet the needs and demands of consumers. Conversely, if the organization's total assets are decreasing, then the company is selling assets. This may mean the firm's executive team is streamlining the company's operations or the firm needs money to meet debt obligations.

As for comparing total assets to sales, for this line item, as investors, we want to see the percent of assets to sales steadily increasing. When this happens, this means that the company is generating more revenues with the same or fewer assets.

Total Assets as a % of Sales				
Balance Sheet				
2018	2017	2016	2015	2014
Total Assets				
5,469	5,292	4,583	5,995	7,101
% of Sales 147.7%	135.5%	151.3%	112.8%	88.5%
Growth 3.3%	15.5%	-23.6%	-15.6%	N/A

Analysis:

The sample company ended 2014 with $7.1 billion in total assets. Their assets then declined in both 2015 and 2016. However, for this decline, the percent of sales as compared to assets increased substantially. In other words, the company was divesting assets, and in doing so, they were able to generate more revenues with fewer assets, from a percentage perspective. In other words, by getting rid of whatever assets they got rid of, they are more efficient as a company.

From a historical perspective, again, as noted above, the organization significantly decreased assets in 2016 and 2015. Specifically, by 15.6% and 23.6% respectively. With this complete, the firm then started to grow assets again at a moderate pace. This shows that the company went through some type of strategic realignment. With this realignment complete in 2016, the firm was unable to set course on a new strategic path. Whether this new path is better or worse, has yet to be seen.

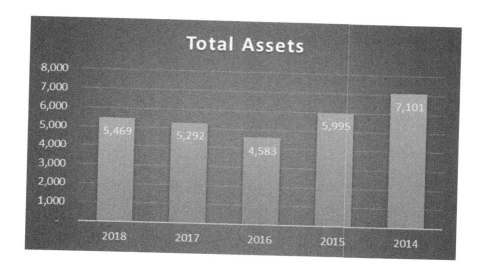

Accounts Payable

The Accounts Payable section of the balance sheet is how much money is owed to suppliers for products or services rendered. The essential trends for this section would be significant fluctuations in the line item. Explicitly, upward trending in this category, concerning the percent of sales, may indicate a shortage in cash supply.

In other words:

When a company buys items that they need to build a product, they are usually given an invoice to pay within a certain amount of time. These funds that are due are considered accounts payable. For the most part, accounts payable needs to be paid within 30 to 60 days after receiving the invoice.

Analysis Tips:

When analyzing accounts payable, the first trend to investigate would be historic. If the organization is continually increasing the size of its Accounts Payable, this could mean the firm is taking longer to pay their suppliers. From this, a closer look at Accounts Payable, as compared to current assets and sales is needed.

A second analysis strategy for accounts payable would be to compare accounts payable concerning sales. If the percentage, compared to sales, is increasing year-over-year, then the company is taking longer to pay their suppliers. This is a good strategy if the organization wishes to utilize their money fully. In other words, if the company can take longer to pay their bills, then the firm has more money to spend on operations.

In contrast, if the organization is paying their accounts payable at a faster pace, then the percent of sales comparison will be declining. When a company does this, they are often taken advantage of early-pay discounts.

Accounts Payable as a % of Sales				
Balance Sheet				
2018	2017	2016	2015	2014
Accounts Payable				
277	249	242	199	233
% of Sales				
3.4%	3.5%	3.5%	2.9%	3.7%

Analysis:

Our firm's Accounts Payable started 2015 with approximately $233 million. As of 2018, Accounts Payable grew to $277 million. In comparing accounts payable with sales, the company had actually declined from 3.7% in 2014 to 3.4% in 2018. This shows the firm may be paying their vendors at a faster pace. For better, or a more precise, picture concerning Accounts Payable, financial ratios are necessitated. Regardless, the company does seem to be staying within a specific margin in relations to sales. This margin is between 3.7% to 2.9%. If the organization begins to fluctuate outside of this range, then a shift in strategy may be hypothesized.

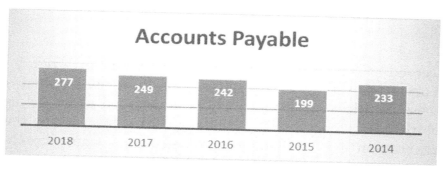

Accrued Expenses

The Accrued Expenses section shows how much money a company is holding in their bank accounts that need to be paid out, relatively soon, for wages and taxes. For example, a company does not pay its employees daily. Instead, they may pay employees on a weekly or biweekly basis. However, wages are accrued continuously. If you think about it, every minute that an employee actually works is wages earned and due by the company.

In other words:

Another way to look at accrued expenses is as a loan from the government or employees. What I mean by this is that the company is holding onto money that is due to the government, taxes, or employees, wages. Until the money is sent to the government or the employees' checks are cashed, a company can use the funds for operational purposes. In other words, the company has free money until employees or government agencies actually cash the checks. With this said, higher accrued expenses are often useful for a company in the short term.

Analysis Tips:

Accrued expenses are not often significantly analyzed by financial analysts. The only time scrutiny is really assessed is when there is a significant increase in accrued expenses, as compared to total assets. This sometimes means that the organization has shifted its pay structure from weekly paychecks to biweekly or monthly checks. This is an excellent strategy to improve net working capital.

Accrued Expenses as a % of Total Assets				
Balance Sheet				
	2018	2017	2016	2015	2014
Accrued Expense	177	151	135	154	126
% of Total Assets	3.2%	2.9%	2.9%	2.6%	1.8%

Analysis:

This company started its 2015 year with $126 million in accrued expenses. The firm then began to trend higher, ending 2018 with $177 million in accrued expenses. Further, as a percent of total assets, the organization ended 2014 at 1.8% of total assets. This increased substantially to 3.2% in 2018. This trend shows that the company is utilizing the 'free money' opportunity by withholding funds in this manner.

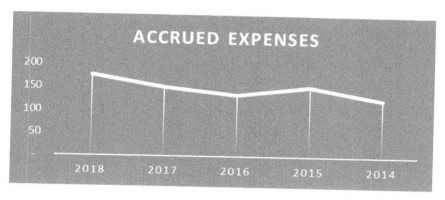

Short-Term Debt

Short-term debt, such as notes payable, are a type of debt that a company must pay within 12 months. This line item will be in the current liabilities section in a balance sheet. Short-term debt may include promissory notes, commercial paper issued, or the current portion due to long-term debt.

In other words:

If the organization has a bank loan payment or bond payment due within the next 12 months, the interest portion will be listed in short-term debt.

Analysis Tips:

For analysis purposes, short-term debt may be evaluated as a percentage of sales, as a percentage of total assets, or even as a percent of equity, which we will examine in the financial ratio section of our book.

Organizations take on short-term debt for numerous reasons. A popular idea is for companies to use debt to cover portions of their current liabilities that current assets will not encompass. In other words, companies are taking on short-term debt because the firm may not be generating enough revenues to pay its bills. This situation is potentially dire for the organization. Without the short-term influx of cash, the organization may not be sustainable in the short term.

If the short-term debt trends, year-over-year, then the organization may have devised specific strategies to exploit using short term debt in operations. Further, this could also represent long-term debt that is coming due within the next 12 months.

When analyzing short-term debt, start with historical trends. If the organization usually carries short-term debt over the long-term, then this may be the standard operating procedure for the firm. If the company had short-term debt and paid it off, then it shows the firm is lowering its debt load. If short-term debt continually increases, then this may indicate the company is regularly having problems meeting its short-term obligations.

Short-term Debt as a % of Sales and Total Assets					
Balance Sheet					
	2018	2017	2016	2015	2014
Short-Term Debt	-	-	-	15	223
% of Sales	0.0%	0.0%	0.0%	0.2%	3.5%

% of Total Assets	0.0%	0.0%	0.0%	0.3%	3.1%

Analysis:

The organization started 2015 with $233 million in short-term debt. At the end of 2015, the company had reduced its debt burden to $15 million. For the last three years, the company has had no reported short-term debt. This shows that the firm may be taking full advantage of low-interest rates and extending their debt repayment past the 12-month cutoff.

Total Current Liabilities

Total current liabilities are how much the company owes to vendors, employees, taxes, and other stakeholders. Typical line items, or categories, within the current liability section includes accounts payable, accrued expenses, accrued taxes, and notes payable. An important commonality between these categories is that any dollar amounts in this section must be repaid within 12 months.

With this as a foundational concept, we can quickly assess that a firm must have equal to or more current assets to cover its current liabilities. Without enough current assets to cover the current liabilities, a company may become insolvent (no money to pay bills) relatively quickly.

As with most things in finance, there are exceptions to this rule. For example, retail and grocery stores tend to have high current liabilities as compared to current assets. This is because competitors in this industry often turn over their inventory a multitude of times within 12 months. This enables the organization to have a continuous cash flow, which allows them to cover current liabilities when they become due.

In other words:

Total current liabilities are all the bills that a company needs to pay within the next 12 months.

Analysis Tips:

When analyzing current liabilities, best practices include comparing the line item with current assets and total assets. Further, trends are essential for this line item. When comparing total liabilities with current assets, we want a percentage below 100%. This shows that the firm has fewer current liabilities as compared to current assets.

If the long-term trend indicates that there are more current liabilities as compared to current assets, then this may be an operational strategy chosen by management and proven effective. However, if this practice happens sporadically, then it may indicate that the company authorizations cash shortfalls.

Current Liabilities as a % Current and Total Assets					
Balance Sheet					
	2018	2017	2016	2015	2014
Current Liabilities	1,384	1,289	1,187	1,197	1,619
% of Current Assets	250.3%	219.6%	144.8%	113.3%	81.9%
% of Total Assets	25.3%	24.4%	25.9%	20.0%	22.8%

Analysis:

Our firm ended 2014 with $1.6 billion in current liabilities. As of the end of 2018, this number declined to $1.3 billion. As for a percentage of total assets though, in 2014, current liabilities were 22.8% of total assets. As of 2018, this had increased to 25.3% of total assets. This shows that the organization is taking on more current liabilities as compared to long-term debt obligations.

From an investor's perspective, the strategy is more than a little concerning. If the economy suddenly slips into a recession, the company may become insolvent relatively quickly. This is especially concerning because the company's current liability almost triples their current assets. This shows that the company significantly relies on a steady stream of cash flows in order to cover their current liabilities. Rather risky.

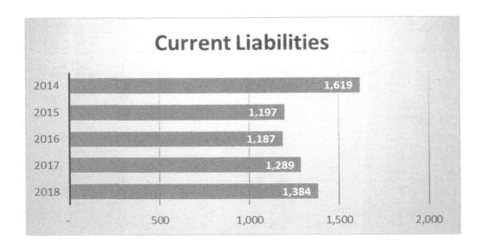

Long Term Debt (LT Debt)

Long-term debt for a company may include promissory notes, bonds, or bank loans. An important characteristic that defines long-term debt is when it needs to be repaid. For long-term debt, this line item is a total amount of funds that must be paid after 12 months.

When using long-term debt, a company is actually making money off of borrowed money. This is a great concept. However, as the company's debt position increases or decreases, so does their risk. This is because the more debt a company has, the more interest they need to pay on a monthly or annual basis. In the event of an economic slowdown, then the higher debt may be the difference between weathering an economic contraction or bankruptcy.

In other words:

Long-term debt is how much money the firm has borrowed and is due to be paid back after 12 months.

Analysis Tips:

In evaluating long-term debt, a critical review must be done with historical trends and the percent of total assets for a company. For historical trends, if the company is continually taking on long-term debt, then the firm is either growing substantially or needs to take on additional funds to support operations. When an organization takes on long-term debt to support operations, this is definitely not a good sign. This shows that the firm is not generating enough revenues to support operations.

About long-term debt, as compared to total assets, this is part of the company's capital structure. In other words, organizations usually target a specific debt load that they prefer to carry when funding future growth. If a consistent trend is identified, then the company can maintain its capital structure. If this percentage is reduced, then it may indicate the firm is trying to reduce its risk by paying off debt.

On the other hand, if the percent of long-term debt increases, as compared to total assets, then the firm is increasing the risk. This action is almost always concerning for investors for the simple fact that the more debt a company takes on, the higher their monthly or annual interest payments. In the event of an economic slowdown, a company is less likely to stay solvent.

Long-term Debt as a % Total Assets					
Balance Sheet					
	2018	2017	2016	2015	2014
Long-Term Debt	926	936	440	1,452	2,481
% of Total Assets	16.9%	17.7%	9.6%	24.2%	34.9%

Analysis:

The company has been seemingly reducing their long-term debt obligations. At the end of 2014, the company had $2.4 billion in long-term debt. As of 2018, their long-term debt position had declined to $926 million. However, what is concerning is that the company seems to be trending higher with debt accumulation over the last few years. In 2016, the organization ended the year with $440 million in debt. This number grew to $936 million in 2017 and $926 million in 2018.

The substantial increase in long-term debt is a smart move, on the one hand. Interest rates are relatively low. By extending long-term debt, the company is taking advantage of the historically low interest rates. On the other hand, significant amounts of debt may hamper their ability to repay principal and interest, if the economy slips into a recession.

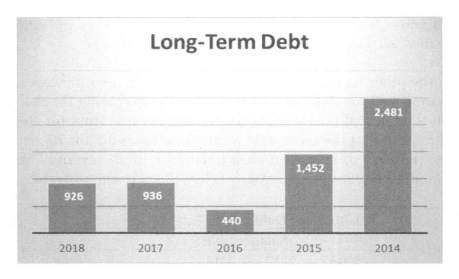

Total Liabilities

Total liabilities include everything and everyone that a company owes money too. Payments of borrowed funds may be made in a relatively short time, current liabilities, or over a more extended period, several years.

The critical ingredient regardless of the firm is paying interest on the borrowed funds or not, is that this money must be paid out. As for a differentiating factor, some forms of liabilities incur interest, while others do not. As noted earlier, accrued taxes and wages are free money for a company, over the short-term, but free money none the less. Whereas, notes and long-term debt must be repaid, with interest.

In other words:

Total liabilities are all the money the company owes to external sources, ranging from employees to long-term debt holders.

Analysis Tips:

As noted above, since total liabilities represent all the funds owed to external sources, this can also be interpreted as total debt for the company. With that said, a comparison with total assets should be examined.

When comparing total liabilities with total assets, a percentage should be used, explicitly dividing total liabilities by total assets. Further, an examination should be done over a 3 to a 5-year term. In this term, if the total liabilities to total assets percentage increases, then the company is taking on additional debt. Again, other debt may be equated with additional risk for the firm.

In contrast, if the percentage decreases over a specific timeframe, then the organization is lowering its financial risk. For the most part, the reduced risk is often appreciated by investors.

Total Liabilities as a % Total Assets					
Balance Sheet					
	2018	2017	2016	2015	2014
Total Liabilities	3,274	3,190	2,630	3,661	4,944
% of Total Assets	59.9%	60.3%	57.4%	61.1%	69.6%

Analysis:

As shown below, the company started off 2015 with $4.9 billion in total liabilities. In 2018, the company decreased their total liabilities to $3.2 billion. This substantial reduction in total liabilities possibly positions the organization to better weather an economic downturn. However, the company has been trending higher with their total liabilities. In 2016, the organization's capital structure started at 57.4% of total assets. This has steadily grown to 59.9% of total assets. This trend starts to reinforce the idea that the company is steadily increasing their debt load. As liabilities increase, so does the organization's risk, overall.

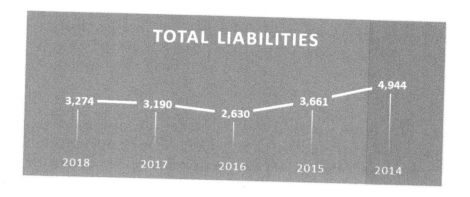

TOTAL LIABILITIES

3,274 — 3,190 — 2,630 — 3,661 — 4,944

2018   2017   2016   2015   2014

Common Stock and Additional Paid-in Capital

The common stock section shown on the balance sheet is a representation of how many shares of stock a company has issued. For simplicity's sake, companies usually value each share at one dollar. As for additional paid-in capital, this represents how much investors paid, above and beyond, the par price. Again, par prices usually are one dollar. By adding together both line items, investors can find the book value for the issued stock.

In other words:

The common stock value represents the number of shares in the market, or available for investors to purchase. Additional paid-in capital is the variable added to common stock to determine the value, or the original price paid for, stock in the open market.

Analysis Tips:

For analysis purposes, we are interested in this line item because the more shares of stock released by a company, frequently, the lower the stock value. This is a straight-up supply and demand concept.

In contrast, if the common stock decreases, this indicates that the company is repurchasing its shares of stock. As a result, the repurchase strategy by the company often increases the overall stock price for the firm.

Common Stock					
Balance Sheet					
	2018	2017	2016	2015	2014
Common Stock	1,631	1,614	1,502	1,405	1,302
Growth	1.1%	7.5%	6.9%	7.9%	N/A

Analysis:

In 2014, the firm had issued 1.3 billion shares of stock. As of 2018, this had increased to 1.3 billion shares. This shows that the company is raising funds by issuing additional equity. As noted above, the strategy will inevitably reduce stock prices because of additional supply in the marketplace as compared to demand. Fortunately, in reviewing the trend below, common stock growth had decreased to 1.1% in 2018. This indicates that the firm may have reached their optimal capital structure.

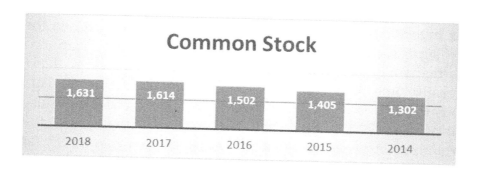

Treasury

Treasury stocks are stock certificates that the company holds for possible later sale. For this line item to *decrease*, a company either needs to issue additional stock shares or repurchase shares of stock from the open market. Of the two likely possibilities, for the most part, treasury accounts *decrease* due to stock repurchases.

In other words:

This one is tricky. Because treasury stock is potential equity one sold, on a balance sheet, is actually listed as a negative number. From this, if the company by stock from the open market, the negative amount would become smaller. For example, -8 may become -10 with a stock buyback.

Analysis Tips:

As investors, we want this line item to go down. When the treasury stock decreases, this indicates that the organization is participating in a stock buyback strategy. However, if the treasury line item stays constant, this is acceptable as well. This means the company is not selling treasury stock to raise funds. Finally, if the treasury stock starts increasing, then the organization is selling its treasury stock to raise funds for operations. Because this action will increase the number of common shares in the open market, his practice often leads to lower stock prices. Not a great deal for shareholders.

Treasury					
Balance Sheet					
	2018	2017	2016	2015	2014
Treasury	(8)	(8)	(8)	(8)	(8)
Growth	0.0%	0.0%	0.0%	0.0%	N/A

Analysis:

In relations to the firm, the company currently has 8 million shares available for disbursement. In other words, if the company needs to raise additional funds, the organization may issue the treasury stocks from their account. In doing this, the organization will be able to quickly raise capital.

In analyzing the statement below, the company has not, significantly, issued or repurchase a large number of stocks. This shows that the firm is using treasury stocks to optimize their capital structure. In any significant way that is.

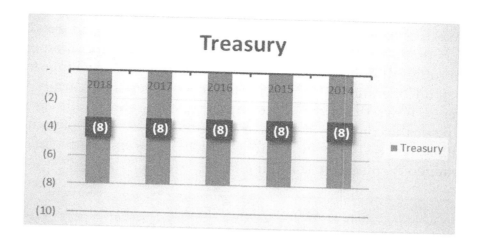

Retained Earnings

Retained earnings are the funds available for the company to use for growth or to start new projects. These funds are the leftovers after expenses and dividends are paid. In general, mature companies tend to use a smaller percentage of net income for retained earning purposes.

In contrast, startup organizations, or companies growing exponentially, will often use all of their net income towards retained earnings. By doing this, companies can avoid accumulating debt and still meet market demands.

In other words:

Net income for a company can either be paid out in dividends or reinvested back into the company in the form of retained earnings.

Analysis Tips:

Investors often look at retained earnings for a change in trend. If retained earnings are increasing, then the organization is forgoing dividend payments to investors and seeking to expand operations. However, a declining retained earnings trend shows that even the company is struggling with cash flow or the company may have increased its dividend payout. Either way, a little bit more research is necessitated when retained earnings are shrinking.

Retained Earnings					
Balance Sheet					
	2018	**2017**	**2016**	**2015**	**2014**
Retained Earnings	658	560	548	1,026	996
Growth	17.4%	2.3%	-46.6%	3.0%	N/A

Analysis:

In the last three years, the company has continually increased their retained earnings. This means that the company is not only increasing their net income, but they are also keeping funds back from investors so they may grow their operations as well.

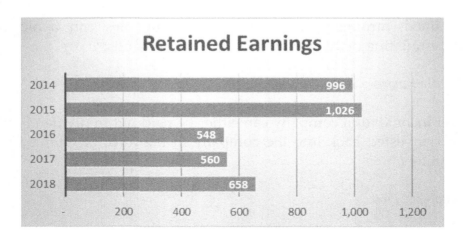

Total Equity

The total equity section of a balance sheet represents how much equity a company uses to fund its assets. As you probably already know this, total equity and total liabilities, as compared to total assets, work in opposite directions. For example, if the company takes on more debt, then their total liabilities will increase, as a percentage of total assets. Further, total equity would decrease, as a percent of total assets. From this, hopefully, you can see that comparing total equity with total assets is a vital analyst strategy.

In other words:

Total equity represents the dollar amount that shareholders would be entitled to after all debts are paid.

Analysis Tips:

A rookie mistake would be to assume investors prefer a high or increasing total equity line item. However, this is not necessarily the case. The higher the total equity, the more investor money is needed to fund operations. From this, a 'rule of thumb' would be for total equity to equal approximately 40 to 45% of total assets. This would indicate a good use of debt but not too much.

Total Equity Balance Sheet					
	2018	2017	2016	2015	2014
Total Equity	2,195	2,102	1,952	2,334	2,157

Growth	4.4%	7.7%	-16.3%	8.2%	N/A
% Total Assets	40.1%	39.7%	42.6%	38.9%	30.4%

Analysis:

In 2014, the company was funding their operations using approximately 30% equity. As of 2018, the company shifted their capital structure to include 40% equity. This shows that the organization is relying more upon equity as compared to debt, in the last several years.

This strategy is helpful if the company wishes to reduce overall risk. However, for growth purposes, this may indicate that the firm is entering a mature business phase and slower growth in revenues and profits should be expected in the near to moderate term.

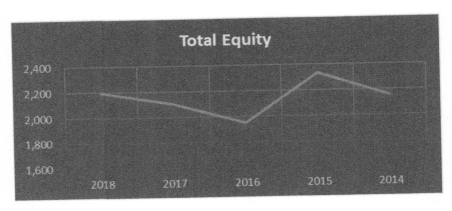

Financial Ratios

Almost every time that I look at a financial statement, I still, even with all my years of educational and professional financial statement analysis experience, get a slight bit overwhelmed with the numbers. This is just one of the many challenges that financial analysis runs into when solely looking at a company's financial statements for insight into their operations and financial performances.

In the grand scheme of financial analysis, reviewing the financial statements alone offers relatively little insight into how a company is performing financially. Granted, by reviewing financial statements alone, we can see if a company is increasing or decreasing the revenues. Further, we are also able to identify, relatively quickly, whether an organization is profitable, by just looking at their net profits. However, in my most humble of opinions, the true essence of financial analysis lies within financial ratios.

The power of financial ratios comes from their ability to show how a company is performing, as a percent of a benchmark. By using percentages, we can compare financial ratios, in a meaningful way, with industry competitors, as well as historically. These comparisons allow us to identify performance and other trends within a company, as well as trends within an industry.

With that said, let us dive into understanding financial ratios. In this section, I start off each segment by broadly defining the ratio category, such as the liquidity ratios, profitability ratios, asset utilization ratios, and debt ratios. Next, a brief definition and concise explanation as to the specific ratios are offered. The final step in the process is showing you how to analyze a particular ratio.

The objective of this process is to walk you through understanding financial ratios, starting with a broad overview, and finishing with tips for analyzing the ratio.

Liquidity Ratios

We all need to pay our bills. In order to do this, we need to ensure that we have enough revenues coming in from our job to cover expenses, usually for the next week or month. The same concept holds true for large and small organizations. Unfortunately, some companies drop the ball in this area.

As investors, we need to make sure that companies are financially solvent (they have enough money to pay their bills over the next twelve months). A great way to determine if a company can meet their short-term obligations is through the use of liquidity ratios.

The objective of these ratios is to help us determine whether a company has enough money coming in over the next 12 months to meet their debt obligations for the same time span (the next twelve months).

Liquidity Ratios Formulas			
Ratio	Numerator	Operation	Denominator
Current Ratio	Current Assets	/	Current Liabilities
Cash Ratio	Cash	/	Current Liabilities
Quick Ratio	Current assets - Inventory	/	Current liabilities
Net Working Capital	(Cash + Inventory + AR)	-	(AP - Accruals)

Liquidity Ratios					
Ratios	2018	2017	2016	2015	2014
Current Ratio	0.40	0.46	0.69	0.88	1.22
Cash Ratio	0.11	0.18	0.23	0.45	0.06
Quick Ratio	0.25	0.32	0.54	0.75	1.10
Net Operating Working Capital	(20)	86	136	423	20

Current Ratio

One of the most popular financial ratios is the current ratio. The current ratio measures the amount of cash inflow (money coming into the company) over the last 12 months with the amount of cash outflow (bills that needed to be paid by the company). From this measurement, we can determine whether the company had enough money coming in to cover funds going out.

Formula:

Current Ratio = Current Assets / Current Liabilities

In the above formula, we can see that if a company has more current assets than current liabilities, the answer will always be higher than one. However, if a company has more current liabilities as compared to current assets, then the answer is going to be less than one.

In other words:

A company has to have more money coming than going out. From this, an organization should have more current assets, dollar-wise, as compared to current liabilities.

Analysis Tips:

A rule of thumb in finance is that if the current ratio is higher than one, then the company is liquid, or financially well off for the short-term. However, if the current ratio falls below one, then there is a reason to be concerned about the organization's liquidity.

Keep in mind; there are ALWAYS exceptions to the rule. For example, grocery stores, and other retail stores, often have a meager, well below one, current ratio. This does not mean that they are financially strained. It is just the nature of the beast in their prospective industry. But again, this is an exception to the rule.

Current Ratio					
	2018	2017	2016	2015	2014
Current Assets	553	587	820	1,056	1,976
/ Current Liabilities	1,384	1,289	1,187	1,197	1,619
Current Ratio	0.40	0.46	0.69	0.88	1.22

Analysis:

In this example, the current ratio started at 1.22 in 2014. However, the company had continually dropped their current ratio to .4 in 2018. This action indicates that the company is maximizing their current assets turnover. This action is common in some industries, such as grocery stores. However, for restaurants, this strategy may be quite risky. Especially, if a recession sets in.

A better strategy for the firm would be to increase their current ratio to industry standards, which is about .7. By doing this, the organization may enjoy moderate liquidity. Further, investors would perceive less risk with the organization. This may inevitably increase stock prices.

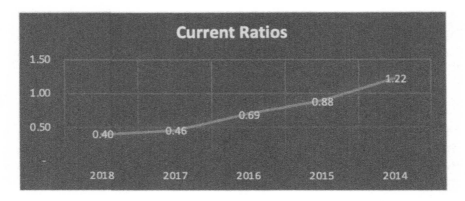

Quick Ratio

The quick ratio is another popular liquidity ratio in the world of finance. This ratio is a modification of the current ratio formula. For the quick ratio, just subtract inventory from current assets THEN divide by the current liabilities. The thought process behind this practice is that inventory, of all the current assets in operations, is the most difficult to liquidate, at least in some industries (ex. it's tough to move an airplane from inventory). As a result, the quick ratio is a little bit better of the measuring stick as to whether a company will have enough funds to meet its 12-month debt obligations.

Formula:

Quick Ratio = (Current Assets – Inventories) / Current Liabilities

In other words:

If a company still has a quick ratio above one, it is really doing well in terms of liquidity.

Analysis Tips:

For the most part, the quick ratio will follow the same trend as the current ratio. However, analysts should pay close attention to how much the quick ratio drops, as compared to the current ratio. If there is a significant reduction in the quick ratio, then an organization may be carrying too much inventory. This may lead to inventory obsolescence or cash flow shortages in the event of an economic contraction. Both bad for the company.

	Quick Ratio				
	2018	**2017**	**2016**	**2015**	**2014**
(Current Asset - Inventory)	553	587	820	1,056	1,976
	205	178	175	163	197
/ Current Liabilities	1,384	1,289	1,187	1,197	1,619
Quick Ratio	0.25	0.32	0.54	0.75	1.10

Analysis:

The firm's quick ratio has followed suit with their current ratio. However, this ratio is actually slightly above industry averages, which is approximately .19. This shows that the company is holding more inventory as compared to their competitors.

To improve this ratio, the firm should reduce their inventory holding. By doing this, the organization will have more cash at their disposal. Further, by reducing inventory, inevitably, the products will increase in quality. This can possibly lead to improved customer satisfaction, as well as, increase liquidity.

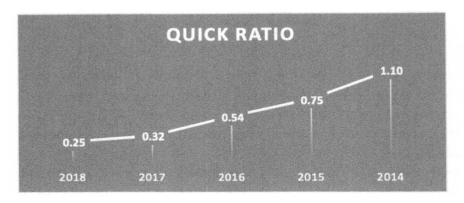

Cash Ratio

When you really want to shake things up, in reference to liquidity ratios, then the cash ratio is the way to do it. As noted above, the current ratio is often considered the industry standard, as to whether a company is sufficiently liquid or not. A more restrictive calculation, to determine the same concept, is the cash ratio. This ratio is more stringent because only cash is included in the calculation.

In this ratio, we are comparing the company's cash to its total current liabilities. If an organization exceeds one, after the calculation is complete, then this means that the company can handle its 12 months debt payments with cash alone.

Formula:

Cash Ratio = Cash / Current Liabilities

In other words:

If a company can pay cash for its debts due in the next 12 months, then liquidity is not a problem.

Analysis Tips:

When analyzing the cash ratio, comparing your target company's cash ratio with industry competitors is almost always the best practice. If the organization is holding more cash, in terms of current liabilities (aka higher cash ratio), as compared to its competitors, then the organization may not be fully utilizing its cash position. What I mean by this is that some of the cash should be transferred into a short-term investment vehicle, such as commercial paper. The logic behind this move is cash sitting in a checking account is not earning any interest. It is just a wasted asset. However, cash invested in short-term securities, such as treasury bills, at least makes some type of return.

Cash Ratio					
	2018	2017	2016	2015	2014
Cash / Current Liabilities	146	233	274	535	98
	1,384	1,289	1,187	1,197	1,619
Cash Ratio	0.11	0.18	0.23	0.45	0.06

Analysis:

The sample company's cash ratio is well below industry averages. This shows that the company, again, relies heavily on current revenues to generate cash. In other words, the company has very little cash reserves.

The theme playing out here is that the company is relying heavily on revenues and revenue growth to meet short-term liquidity needs. In the event of a recession, the organization may find borrowing costs significantly higher due to their stringent cash buffer policies.

Asset Ratios

Here is a thought, what if we can make the same amount of money from our business, in revenues, with a small building as compared to a large one? If this is possible, then our business, if operating from a large building, is not utilizing our assets effectively. In other words, we are wasting money on the large building because the small building would work just dandy. Unfortunately, small and large corporations do this all the time. Underutilizing their assets, that is.

In order for us, as investors, to determine whether a company is wasting their money on underutilized assets, we can employ various asset ratios. Popular asset management ratios include inventory turnover, total asset turnover and many more.

In the simplest terms, asset ratios measure how efficient a company's managerial team is utilizing its scarce resources, specifically assets. In some instances, these ratios may not mean much by themselves. However, they may be quite powerful when compared to industry competitors.

Asset Utilization			
Ratios	**Numerator**	**Operation**	**Denominator**
Total Asset Turnover	Sales	/	Total Assets
Fixed Asset Turnover	Sales	/	Fixed Assets
Days Sales Outstanding	Accounts Receivable	/	(Annual sales / 365)
Inventory	Sales	/	Inventory

Turnover			
Accounts Receivable Turnover	Sales	/	Accounts Receivable
Working Capital Turnover	Sales	/	Working Capital
AP Turnover	Sales	/	Accounts Payable
Average Days Inventory	Inventory Turnover	/	365
Average Days Payable	AP Turnover	/	365

Asset Utilization					
Ratios	2018	2017	2016	2015	2014
Total Asset Turnover	1.48	1.35	1.51	1.13	0.89
Fixed Asset Turnover	3.33	3.16	3.40	2.10	1.86
Days Sales Outstanding	3.75	3.82	3.37	4.21	4.88
Inventory Turnover	39.41	40.28	39.62	41.50	31.90
Accounts Receivable Turnover	97.35	95.60	108.33	86.72	74.82
Working Capital Turnover	(404.00)	83.37	50.98	15.99	314.25
AP Turnover	29.17	28.80	28.65	33.99	26.97
Average Days Inventory	0.11	0.11	0.11	0.11	0.09
Average Days Payable	0.08	0.08	0.08	0.09	0.07

Total Asset Turnover

The total asset turnover ratio shows how much revenues a company generates in terms of its assets utilized.

Formula:

Total Asset Turnover = Sales / Total Assets

In other words:

The ratio helps investors understand how much total asset was needed for the company to generate the revenues.

Analysis Tips:

For the most part, the lower the total assets and the higher the sales, the better. As a result, an optimal trend for this ratio would be an increasingly larger number for total asset turnover, year-over-year. This would show that the company is generating more revenues with the same or fewer assets.

Total Asset Turnover					
	2018	2017	2016	2015	2014
Sales	8,080	7,170	6,933	6,764	6,285
/ Total Assets	5,469	5,292	4,583	5,995	7,101
Total Asset Turnover	1.48	1.35	1.51	1.13	0.89

Analysis:

The firm's total asset turnover had increased substantially over the last five years. This means that the company is better utilizing their assets as compared to sales. In 2014, the company's total asset turnover was .89. In the next three years, this would increase to 1.13, 1.15, and 1.35. As of last year, the total asset turnover reached 1.48. This trend indicates that the company has taken steps to maximize its fixed assets. If this trend continues, investors can rest assure that future assets will be highly leveraged and optimally used.

Fixed Asset Turnover

The same concept holds true for fixed asset turnover ratio, as for the total asset turnover ratio, which is the fewer assets, in this case, fixed assets used to generate revenues the better. This is because the company is spending less money on property, plant, and equipment to generate more revenues.

The object of this ratio is to determine whether a company is fully utilizing its property, plant, and equipment to generate revenues. For this analysis, a review of historical trends, as well as comparing it to industry competitors, are excellent choices for financial analysis.

Formula:

Fixed Asset Turnover = Sales / Fixed Assets.

In other words:

This ratio answers the question: "Does the company really need all of the toys that they have?" or better yet "are they playing with all of their toys?".

Analysis Tips:

If the fixed asset turnover is decreasing, then the organization is using more fix assets to generate the same amount of revenues. Not a good situation. This may mean that the company had bought too many pieces of equipment or buildings, and they are not being used that much. Or, the organization's revenues are slowing down, and they now have access to excess capacity. A great way to make this determination is through a historical review of the ratio. In other words, check out the trend.

Fixed Asset Turnover					
	2018	2017	2016	2015	2014
Sales	8,080	7,170	6,933	6,764	6,285
/ Fixed Assets	2,429	2,272	2,041	3,215	3,381
Fixed Asset Turnover	3.33	3.16	3.40	2.10	1.86

Analysis:

The same theme is playing out for fixed asset turnover as compared to total asset turnover. Specifically, fixed asset turnover had increased from 1.86 in 2014 to 3.33 in 2018. This trend is well above industry averages. Quite frankly, I am not sure if this ratio can improve any further. Management is doing a fantastic job of utilizing assets.

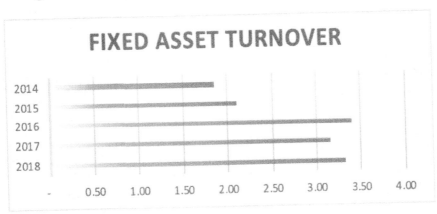

Days Sales Outstanding

The days' sales outstanding shows investors how long it takes a company to collect funds from the sale of their products or services. The quicker a company can collect its money, the quicker they can reinvest the funds into operations. Thus, a low day count is optimal.

In working through this formula, make sure to first divide annual sales by 365. Next, divide accounts receivable by the denominator. This step will give you days sales outstanding.

Formula:

$$DSO = Accounts\ Receivable\ /\ Annual\ Sales\ /\ 365$$

In other words:

The sooner a company can collect the money owed to them, the better off they are.

Analysis Tips:

From an analysis perspective, this ratio tells investors how efficient the company's collection department operates. Further, this may also indicate how 'loose' a company is with its credit policy. What I mean by this is that some companies allow retailers or vendors to take their sweet time in paying their invoices. This is helpful for vendors because they can use the cash for other purposes. This is not so great for the target organization because they have less cash to use in operations or investing.

From this, days sales outstanding should be declining as a trend or lower than competitors' comparable ratios.

Days Sales Outstanding					
	2018	2017	2016	2015	2014
Accounts Receivable	83	75	64	78	84
/ Annual Sales	8,080	7,170	6,933	6,764	6,285
/365	365	365	365	365	365
Days Sales Outstanding	3.75	3.82	3.37	4.21	4.88

Analysis:

The days' sales outstanding for the target company started at 4.87 in 2014. This ratio decreased substantially over the last five years. In 2018, this ratio was down to 3.75. This means that the company is taking longer to collect on its accounts receivable. As a restaurant, this ratio should not be too worrisome.

Inventory Turnover

The inventory turnover ratio tells investors how many times a company was able to cycle through their inventory stock. As with most asset utilization ratios, this calculation is best analyzed using historical records, as well as, competitors' comparable ratios.

Formula:

$$Inventory\ Turn = Sales / Inventory$$

In other words:

As for a rule of thumb, the more times that a company cycles through its inventory, the better. This is because the organization can keep their inventory low and replenish inventory items when needed.

Analysis Tips:

Inventory turnover ratios are best analyzed through competitor comparison or historical trends. If your target company's inventory turnover ratio is lower than competitors, then they are carrying too much inventory on an annual basis. As for historical trends, investors love to see the inventory turnover ratio continually increasing over time. This shows that the firm is carrying fewer products. This helps to avoid inventory obsolescence.

Inventory Turnover					
	2018	**2017**	**2016**	**2015**	**2014**
Sales	8,080	7,170	6,933	6,764	6,285
/ Inventory	205	178	175	163	197
Inventory Turnover	**39.41**	**40.28**	**39.62**	**41.50**	**31.90**

Analysis:

The company's inventory turnover started at 31.49 in 2014. In 2015, their inventory turnover increased to 41.5. Over the next three years, this ratio as kept relatively close to 40. This indicates that the company is maintaining a specific level of inventory over an extended period. In other words, this trend is not an accident. Evidently management feels that to keep quality products, this ratio needs to be upheld.

Based on the company's effectiveness with fixed asset management, I would respect their judgment. However, if this trend changes in the future, then a closer look at management effectiveness must be done.

Accounts Receivable Turnover

The accounts receivable turnover tells investors how many times the company was able to collect funds from retailers and direct buyers. In some instances, when the company has no accounts receivable, or a very low value, this calculation may be overlooked.

Formula:

AR Turnover = Sales / Accounts Receivable

In other words:

Just because a company is selling products does not mean that they get paid for it. At least in a timely manner.

Analysis Tips:

Accounts receivable turnover is best scrutinized using their historical trend. If an organization keeps a steady, or constant, accounts receivable turnover, then the management team is executing its accounts receivable strategy consistently. For the most part, this is good. If this ratio increases, then the organization is becoming more efficient with their Accounts Receivable collections.

In contrast, if this ratio starts to fall, then the organization may be loosening their credit terms or failing to collect funds due on time. Either way, more research is needed on the part of the investor to determine if the strategy is good or not so good.

Account Receivable Turnover					
	2018	2017	2016	2015	2014
Sales	8,080	7,170	6,933	6,764	6,285
/ Accounts Receivable	83	75	64	78	84
Account Receivable Turnover	97.35	95.60	108.33	86.72	74.82

Analysis:

The sample firm's accounts receivable turnover started at 75 in 2014. This ratio had gradually increased to 97.35 in 2018. This shows that the organization is continually improving their accounts receivable collection. Again, as a restaurant, this ratio is only moderately important.

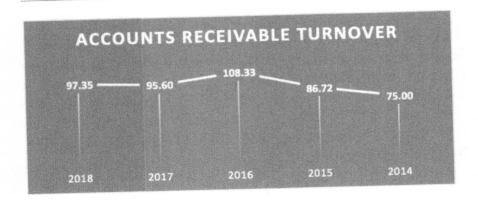

Accounts Payable Turnover

Accounts payable turnover tells us how many times a company paid out its average accounts' payable dollar amount on an annual basis. The objective of reviewing this ratio is to find out how quickly our company is paying its debt to suppliers.

Formula:

$$AP\ Turnover = Sales / Accounts\ Payable$$

In other words:

Goldilocks and the Three Bears come to mind. Companies that are paying accounts payable too quick show a lack of utilization with working capital. Firms that wait too long risk jeopardizing their credit with their vendors. Now paying their accounts payable in a consistent manner is optimal for investors.

Analysis Tips:

A slow paying company often indicates a cash shortage. Whereas a company quickly paying their accounts payable may suggest that the firm lacks optimal exploitation of accounts payable funds. In other words, the company could be holding onto funds due to suppliers a little bit longer.

	Account Payable Turnover				
	2018	2017	2016	2015	2014
Sales	8,080	7,170	6,933	6,764	6,285
/ Accounts Payable	277	249	242	199	233
Account Payable Turnover	29.17	28.80	28.65	33.99	26.97

Analysis:

This company's Accounts Payable turnover started at 26.96 in 2014. In 2015, this ratio jumped up to 34.02. However, over the last three years, this ratio has leveled out at approximately 29. This indicates that the company has a strategic plan set up to maximize accounts payable usage. Because this trend is over several years, investors may rest assured that this ratio may very well may be optimized. From this, a decrease in this ratio trend may indicate a change in strategy. With any change in policy, a closer review is often warranted.

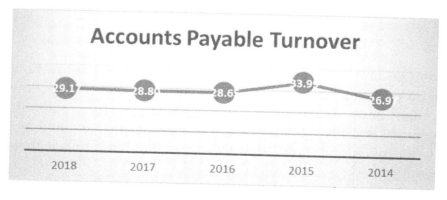

Accounts Payable Turnover

Other Asset Ratio Calculations

Working Capital Turnover

Working capital turnover tells investors how well a company is exploiting its working capital opportunities. The higher the working capital turnover, the more efficient the management team is utilizing their working capital funds.

Working Capital Turnover					
	2018	2017	2016	2015	2014
Sales	8,080	7,170	6,933	6,764	6,285
/ Working Capital	(20)	86	136	423	20
Working Capital Turnover	(404.00)	83.37	50.98	15.99	314.25

Average Days in Inventory

Average days in inventory is a measurement related to how long a company takes to sell, or move, their inventory. Low average days in inventory means that the firm sells its inventory quickly. In contrast, a higher number for average days of inventory shows that the firm takes time to sell their inventory.

Average Days in Inventory					
	2018	2017	2016	2015	2014
Inventory Turnover	39	40	40	41	32
/ 365	365	365	365	365	365
Average Days in Inventory	**0.11**	**0.11**	**0.11**	**0.11**	**0.09**

Average Days Payable

The average days payable is a measurement focused on how long a company takes to pay its current bills. In other words, how long does the firm take to pay their electric bill? The higher than average days payable, the longer the company takes to pay. In some instances, this action is preferable because the company may use the funds for operating purposes.

Average Days Payable					
	2018	2017	2016	2015	2014
Accounts Payable Turnover	29.17	28.80	28.65	33.99	26.97
/ 365	365	365	365	365	365
Average Days Payable	**0.08**	**0.08**	**0.08**	**0.09**	**0.07**

Profitability Ratios

For some unknown reason (ha, ha, ha) investors are interested in profits. Because of this essential topic, finance professionals have come up with various profitability ratios. These ratios take a look at a company's profits from different perspectives. For example, the return on equity ratio analyzes a company's returns as compared to equity investments in the company. By reviewing profits from different angles, investors can have a well-rounded understanding of the profitability of an organization.

Profitability Ratios			
Ratios	Numerator	Operation	Denominator
Return on Assets	Net income	/	Total Assets
Return on Equity	Net income	/	Equity
Net Profit Margin	Net Income	/	Sales
Gross Profit Margin	(Revenues - COGS)	/	Revenues
Operating Profit Margin	EBIT	/	Sales
Basic Earning Power	EBIT	/	Total Assets
ROCE	EBIT	/	Total Assets - Current Lab.
Capital Employed	Total Assets	-	Current Liabilities
ROIC	NOPAT	/	Operating

				Capital

Profitability Ratios					
Ratios	2018	2017	2016	2015	2014
Return on Assets	10.90%	9.05%	8.18%	11.83%	4.03%
Return on Equity	27.15%	22.79%	19.21%	30.38%	13.26%
Net Profit Margin	7.38%	6.68%	5.41%	10.48%	4.55%
Gross Profit Margin	71.50%	71.13%	70.59%	69.18%	69.90%
Operating Profit Margin	9.48%	9.44%	8.97%	2.59%	2.77%
Basic Earning Power	14.01%	12.79%	13.57%	2.92%	2.45%
ROCE	18.75%	16.91%	18.32%	3.65%	3.17%
Capital Employed	4,085	4,003	3,396	4,798	5,482
ROIC	28.54%	21.77%	25.52%	4.29%	4.59%

Return on Assets (ROA)

In keeping with the profitability thing, the return on assets allows investors to assess how profitable our target organization is as compared to the total assets utilized by the organization. With this ratio, investors prefer to see a relatively high return on assets. This indicates that the organization is generating net profits from assets as a whole.

Formula:

$$ROA = Net\ Income\ /\ Total\ Assets$$

In other words:

This ratio shows us how much profits the company was able to generate using all the assets of their organization.

Analysis Tips:

In reviewing this from a trend perspective, a continually increasing return on assets is preferred. Further, comparisons with other competitors within the industry may also help investors gain a better view.

If the company is continually increasing its return on assets, then the company is making more profits using the same amount or fewer assets. In contrast, if the company's return on assets is decreasing, then the firm is making fewer profits as compared to their assets used within the organization.

Return on Assets					
	2018	2017	2016	2015	2014
Net Income	596	479	375	709	286
/ Total Assets	5,469	5,292	4,583	5,995	7,101
Return on Assets	10.90%	9.05%	8.18%	11.83%	4.03%

Analysis:

The company's return on assets ended 2014 horribly at 4.03%. In 2015, possibly after the sale of Red Lobster (as noted earlier, this example is from Darden Restaurants), this ratio jumped up to 11.83%. In 2016, the return on assets fell to 8.18%. However, in the last three years, the company's return on assets has gradually increased to 10.9% in 2018. This shows that the company is continually optimizing their return on assets. Once this ratio levels off, optimization may be reached. In other words, the company may still be optimizing its asset usage... room for improvement.

Return on Equity (ROE)

Almost all investors are crazy about return on equity. This is because the return on equity indicates to investors how much the company profited in relation to equity invested. As shown below, the calculation for return on equity is net income divided by total equity. Investors want to see this ratio as high as possible and climbing, over time. This is because either a company is increasing its net income by using the same amount of equity invested or the firm is using less equity to generate the same amount of money.

Formula:

ROE = Net Income / Total Equity

In other words:

The return on equity indicates how much profits were earned by a company in relation to equity invested.

Analysis Tips:

When analyzing the return on equity, investors prefer to see a high return on equity. Further, investors prefer to see the return on equity increase over time. This shows that the organization is making money from investors' investments. On a side note, if a company's return on equity is significantly higher as compared to competitors, then the organization may be taking on additional debt to fund operations as compared to equity. This is risky because the more debt that a company takes on, the more susceptible they are to bankruptcy.

Return on Equity					
	2018	2017	2016	2015	2014
Net Income	596	479	375	709	286
Equity					

	2,195	2,102	1,952	2,334	2,157
Return on Equity	**27.15%**	**22.79%**	**19.21%**	**30.38%**	**13.26%**

Analysis:

In the last three years, the organization has continually improved its return on equity. In 2016, their return on equity was 19.2%. The industry average is 14.77%. As of 2018, return on equity reached 27.16%. This shows the organization is exploiting its debt opportunities and wisely balancing their capital budgeting structure.

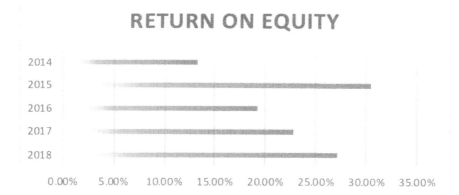

Net Profit Margin

My personal favorite financial ratio is the profit margin. The profit margin ratio compares a company's net income, or profits, with their revenues. Again, the higher this ratio, the better for investors. A distressing trend to be mindful of, as an investor, is when the profit margin increases when revenues fall. This happens because management has taken it upon themselves to cut costs within the company significantly. Unfortunately, this type of action is not sustainable. Further, cost-cutting often leads to long-term revenue decline.

Formula:

Profit Margin = Net Income / Total Revenues

In other words:

If you want to see how well a management team is doing, check out the company's profit margins. This is because just about all line items between revenues and net profits are under the control of the company's management team. Increasing net profits are fantastic. Declining net profits, over time, disturbing.

Analysis Tips:
Profit margins are best analyzed using historical trends. If the company is continually increasing their profit margins, then this is a great situation. Another acceptable trend would be a steady profit margin. This would indicate that an organization is keeping its costs in line with revenues. As you probably already guessed, a concerning trend would be a shrinking profit margin.

Net Profit Margin					
	2018	2017	2016	2015	2014
Net Income	596	479	375	709	286

| Sales | 8,080 | 7,170 | 6,933 | 6,764 | 6,285 |
| Net Profit Margin | 7.38% | 6.68% | 5.41% | 10.48% | 4.55% |

Analysis:

In the last three years, the firm's profit margin has increased from 5.4% to 7.38%. Not only is the organization continually increasing the revenues, but they are also maintaining a healthy net profit growth. By doing this, the organization will possibly have plenty of funds for dividend payments, as well as funding future growth opportunities.

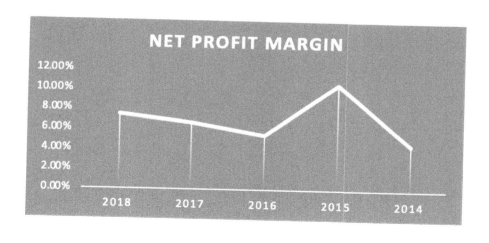

Gross Profit Margin

The gross profit margin tells investors, in percentage form, how much funds are available after raw materials are paid. The higher the gross profit margins, the more money available to pay for other costs within the company.

Formula:

Gross Profit Margin = (Revenues – COGS) / Revenues

In other words:

The gross profit margin shows the percentage amount that a company pays for raw material as compared to revenues.

Analysis Tips:

If the gross profit margin continually shrinks, then this indicates that either price for raw material is increasing substantially and costs are not being transferred to customers. Or, management is not doing an outstanding job with negotiating prices from suppliers. This would then indicate that suppliers have significant power in this relationship.

Gross Profit Margin					
	2018	**2017**	**2016**	**2015**	**2014**
(Revenues	8,080	7,170	6,933	6,764	6,285
- COGS)	2,303	2,070	2,039	2,085	1,892
/ Revenues	8,080	7,170	6,933	6,764	6,285
Gross Profit Margin	**71.50%**	**71.13%**	**70.59%**	**69.18%**	**69.90%**

Analysis:

The firm started 2014 with a gross profit margin of 69.9%. The organization has been able to slightly improve this ratio. In 2018, their gross profit margin is now 71.5%. Quite possibly, in the near term, this ratio should stabilize. This would indicate a maximized gross profit margin. With this reach, the organization should be an industry leader in this regard.

Gross Profit Margin

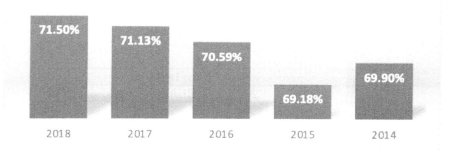

2018	2017	2016	2015	2014
71.50%	71.13%	70.59%	69.18%	69.90%

Operating Profit Margin

The operating profit margin helps investors understand how much money, from the perspective of operations, that a company is generating, as compared to total sales for the same timeframe. This ratio is a great indicator of how well the company's management team is performing.

Formula:

Operating Profit Margin = EBIT / Revenues

In other words:

The operating profit margin only looks at costs directly related to operations and compares them with sales. This ratio helps to eliminate attempts by management to impact the bottom line, or profit margin, through events not related to a company's core operations, like selling investment securities.

Analysis Tips:

If an organization can maintain steady operating profit margins, then the organization may be deemed relatively low risk. Fluctuations in this ratio could indicate cost-cutting measures or lax management oversight.

Operating Profit Margin					
	2018	2017	2016	2015	2014
EBIT	766	677	622	175	174
/ Sales	8,080	7,170	6,933	6,764	6,285
Operating Profit Margin	9.48%	9.44%	8.97%	2.59%	2.77%

Analysis:

In 2015 and 2014, the company's operating profit margin was approximately 2.6%. After alleviating the organization of some of their underperforming assets, seemingly, their operating profit margin skyrocketed to between 9% to 9 ½%. This indicates that management is doing an excellent job generating revenues using minimal operating assets.

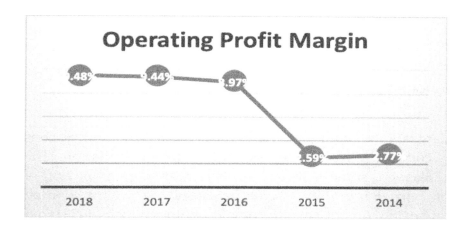

Debt Ratios

Organizations love to use debt. There are two main reasons why companies embrace the action of debt accumulation. The first reason is some managers excel with making money off of debt. In doing this, equity investors are well rewarded because they do not have to come up with a bunch of cash out of pocket. If a company wishes to grow, or invest in a new project, just let managers borrow money. A second reason why businesses love debt is that interest payments are often tax-deductible. From this, using debt is usually significantly cheaper than equity.

Any time that I discuss debt with students or clients, I like the use the phrase that 'some debt, like chocolate cake, is good. However, too much debt, again, like chocolate cake, is not better'. As a company accumulates more debt, they are also accumulating leverage or risk. As a company's risk increases, then the cost of borrowing will inevitably increase as well. This will lead to increased interest payments.

In the event of economic turndown, elevated interest payments are often hard to manage. Making these payments is often the difference between bankruptcy or weathering a recession.

Because of the importance of understanding a company's debt position, financial professionals love to employ three specific ratios geared towards debt. The ratios are the long-term debt ratio, debt to equity ratio, and times interest earned.

Debt Ratios			
Ratios	Numerator	Operation	Denominator
Debt Ratio	LT Debt	/	Total Assets
Debt/Equity	LT Debt	/	Common Equity
Times Interest Earned	EBIT	/	Interest Expense

Long-term Debt					
Ratios	2018	2017	2016	2015	2014
Debt Ratio	16.93%	17.69%	9.60%	24.22%	34.94%
Debt/Equity	42.19%	44.53%	22.54%	62.21%	115.02%
Times Interest Earned	4.76	16.93	3.62	0.91	1.30

Long-Term Debt Ratio

The long-term debt ratio compares a company's long-term debt with total assets. The higher this percentage, the more a company uses debt for funding their operations.

Formula:

$$LT\ Debt\ Ratio = LT\ Debt / Total\ Assets.$$

In other words:

The long-term debt ratio tells investors how well a company manages its debt usage.

Analysis Tips:

As we all know, there are only two ways to finance a company. They are debt or equity. If a company has a high long-term debt ratio, then the firm is highly leveraged. In other words, the organization faces substantial risk because of its obligations to repay the principal and interest on the debt borrowed. As noted before, this situation often creates peril in the event of a revenue decline or overall economic slowdown.

In contrast, the company has an incredibly low, or no, debt ratio; then this means that the organization is operating based on all equity. This situation can more than piss off investors because of the opportunities available for debt exploitation.

Long-Term Debt Ratio					
	2018	2017	2016	2015	2014
LT Debt	926	936	440	1,452	2,481
/ Total Assets	5,469	5,292	4,583	5,995	7,101
Long-Term Debt Ratio	16.93%	17.69%	9.60%	24.22%	34.94%

Analysis:

In 2014, the firms seemed to be burdened with significant long-term debt. Specifically, the company's debt ratio, long-term, was 35.95%. Granted, this is definitely below industry averages. However, the organization was able to significantly reduce their debt load over the next two years. This resulted in a long-term debt ratio of 9.6% in 2016. Gradually, over the next two years, the company has taken on some more debt. At the end of 2018, their long-term debt ratio was sitting at 16.93%.

Since interest rates have been gradually rising over the last couple of years, the organization may want to consider taking on additional debt and possibly targeting a 20% long-term debt ratio. This will allow the company to exploit low-interest rates, while maintaining a relatively moderate debt ratio.

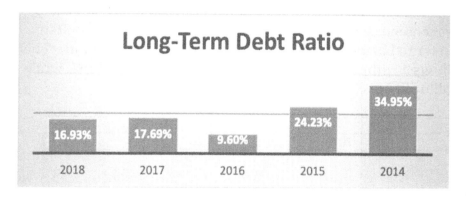

Debt to Equity Ratio

The debt to equity ratio indicates how much debt is used, as compared to, equity. This is just another way of looking at the use of debt for a company. For me, I will calculate the debt ratio 100 times before I will calculate the debt-to-equity ratio, for financial analysis purposes. Just because this calculation is better used for other financial analysis tools, such as calculating the weighted average cost of capital.

Formula:

Debt to Equity Ratio = LT Debt / Total Equity

In other words:

This ratio shows investors a good comparison between debt and equity.

Analysis Tips:

Surprisingly, an accessible debt to equity ratio would be a percentage close to 100. This is because organizations often prefer to balance their debt and equity in equal amounts. This allows a company to take on a moderate amount of risk while still utilizing caution.

Debt to Equity Ratio					
	2018	2017	2016	2015	2014
LT Debt	926	936	440	1,452	2,481
/ Total Equity	2,195	2,102	1,952	2,334	2,157
Debt to Equity Ratio	42.19%	44.53%	22.54%	62.21%	115.02%

Analysis:

The company ended 2014 with a debt to equity ratio of 115.04%. In other words, the organization had a whole bunch of debt. However, this was about average for the restaurant industry. In the next four years, the company would decrease their debt to equity position to 22.54%. In the last two years, the company has increased its debt-to-equity ratio to between 42 to 44.5%.

The stabilization of the debt-to-equity ratio over the last two years indicates that the company has a specific capital structure target. By maintaining an optimal capital structure, the company can reach a maintainable weighted average cost of capital.

DEBT TO EQUITY RATIO

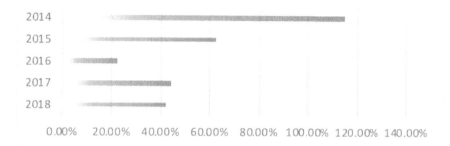

Times Interest Earned

Times Interest Earned

Times interest earned is a biggie for banks and other lenders. This is because the ratio compares interest expenses with operating income. The higher this ratio, the more likely a company is to be able to afford their interest payments.

Formula:

$$TIE = EBIT / Interest\ Expenses$$

In other words:

If you are a banker, then examine this ratio. If not, move on to more informative ratios.

Analysis Tips:

This ratio should be analyzed when an investor is concerned about a company's debt load. If this ratio continually trends higher, then an organization is continuously increasing the risk. In contrast, if this trend declines, then this indicates that an organization is paying off its debt.

Times Interest Earned					
	2018	2017	2016	2015	2014
EBIT	766	677	622	175	174
/ Interest Expense	161	40	172	192	134
Times Interest Earned	4.76	16.93	3.62	0.91	1.30

Analysis:

Of all of the firm's financial ratios, this one is most peculiar. In 2014, their times interest earned ratio was 1.3. In the next year, this ratio felt the .91. This indicates that the company barely had enough funds to meet its interest payments. In subsequent years, this ratio has significantly fluctuated between 16.3 and 3.6.

The reason for this fluctuation could be how the company has their debt repayment structured. As an investor, we should be worried and do further research in relations to their debt restructure payments. Predictable debt repayment structures allow for transparency and planning. Unpredictable debt repayment structures inherently increase risk exposure for investors.

Financial Ratio Summary

As with most organizations, this organization has its share of strengths and weaknesses, in relation to its financial ratios.

Financial Ratio Strengths

Of all their financial ratios, the company's most impressive statistics lie within their asset utilization. For my calculations, the company is doing amazingly well with utilizing their total assets. Further, this should allow the company to have reached an industry-leading position.

Financial Ratio Challenges

As for challenges, the company is really playing hard and fast with its cash position. One miscalculation and the organization may be paying significantly higher interest rates to borrow funds to cover emergencies or unexpected costs/revenue decline.